YOU NEVER BE SICK AGAIN

GOD'S PROVISION FOR HEALTH AND WHOLENESS

TONY O AKPATI

YOU SHALL NEVER BE SICK AGAIN

The First Edition 2019

Copyright @ 2019 Anthony O. Akpati

ISBN- 978-0-9913641-3-8

No part of this manuscript may be reproduced or transmitted in any form or by any means, electronic or mechanical, including photocopying, printing, recording, or by any information storage and retrieval system, without the written permission of the author. For further information contact the Author.

Unless otherwise noted, all scripture is from the King James Version of the Bible © 1982 by Thomas Nelson, Inc. Used by permission. Scripture quotations marked NKJV are from the New King James Version of the Bible.

The King's House Publications of The King's House Ministries.

Email: info@thekingshouselive.org, toniakpati@yahoo.com

Website: www.thekingshouselive.org

Table of Contents

Introduction 1

Preface 4

Chapter One: The Need For Salvation 7

Chapter Two: God's Will Is Total Health 18

Chapter Three: Spirit, Soul And Body 26

Chapter Four: Living By The Word 33

Chapter Five: The Place Of Faith 39

Chapter Six: Stay Away From Sin 56

Chapter Seven: Deal With Toxic Emotions 60

Chapter Eight: The Gateway Of The Mind 75

Chapter Nine: The Need For Spirituality 81

Chapter Ten: Provision For Healing 85

Chapter Eleven: Habits For Healthy Living 88

INTRODUCTION

By way of introduction I want to lay the foundation that will help you to understand the subject addressed in this book so as to take delivery of your total health inheritance.

In our world today the idea that anyone can live without sickness without depending on prescription drugs or medications sounds incredible. This is because we have drifted too far away from God's original intention for mankind, his plans, his purpose and provisions. We as humans have gotten to the point that we don't consider God's ways in anything we do. Interestingly, there is God's provision for sickness-free living. That is what I will be sharing in this book. Paul the Apostle asked King Agrippa and the Jews a pertinent question while speaking about the resurrection of the dead. He said, *"Why should it be thought a thing incredible with you, that God should raise the dead?"*(Acts 26:8). We tend to put God in the class of man. Man is not a match for God in any sense. God is the creator while man is the creature.

And Jesus looking upon them saith, With men it is impossible, but not with God: for with God all things are possible.

Mark 10:27

No doubt, the medical profession is doing a great deal in terms of saving lives. However, with all due respect, I want to make this humble submission that medical practice is limited in scope. If medical science has all the answers to the issue of health, then the medical doctors and all the medical practitioners should be the healthiest of all humans. But that is not the case. Think about that! I went to see a doctor for my yearly physical not long ago. It was my first time at that office. So, they gave me a bunch of paper work to fill out. Reading through the waiver, I found this interesting statement; "The practice of medicine is not an exact science, the result of the treatment is not guaranteed." No wonder it is called medical practice. This goes to show that there is something more we need to know, and that is the God factor. Without including God in this discussion, living a sickness-free life remains an illusion. Let no one fool you. Education is good but education without God is dangerous. There are two sides to education; the academic and the spiritual. The majority of people are only conversant with the academic and they have no clue about spiritual education. They are more or less novices and spiritual illiterates when it comes to spiritual education. I don't mean to slight anyone's intelligence. Permit me to say at this point: "all you know is not all there is." It will take humility for one to learn new things, and God only teaches the teachable.

Good and upright is the Lord: therefore will he teach sinners in the way. The meek will he guide in judgment: and the meek will he teach his way.

Psalms 25:8-9

A wise man will hear, and will increase learning; and a man of understanding shall attain unto wise counsels.

Proverbs 1:5

Part of the reason why health concerns have remained a major problem today is because we have limited ourselves to academic education.

And ye shall know the truth, and the truth shall make you free.

John 8:32

I pray that your heart be opened to receive the truth that will make you free from every form of oppression of the spirit of infirmity in Jesus mighty name. Amen!

PREFACE

Sickness and disease was not part of the human condition at the time of creation. Let's consider what God intended Eden to be like. Let's imagine God's intention when he created Eden. Adam and Eve were living a super healthy life before the advent of sin. Sickness and disease were introduced into the world as one of the consequences of sin after the fall of man in the Garden of Eden. The fact that humans are plagued with all kinds of sickness and disease was not the case from the beginning of creation.

And the Lord God commanded the man, saying, Of every tree of the garden thou mayest freely eat: But of the tree of the knowledge of good and evil, thou shalt not eat of it: for in the day that thou eatest thereof thou shalt surely die.

Genesis 2:16-17

Man literally brought sickness and disease unto himself by disregarding the instructions of God.

Hast thou not procured this unto thyself, in that thou hast forsaken the Lord thy God, when he led thee by the way

Jeremiah 2:17

It is absolutely impossible to live a super healthy life without following the precepts of the word of God. I believe that you will agree with me that the manufacturer of any product knows more about the product than any other person. That's right! God is the one that made man; spirit, soul and body.

And God said, Let us make man in our image, after our likeness: and let them have dominion over the fish of the sea, and over the fowl of the air, and over the cattle, and over all the earth, and over every creeping thing that creepeth upon the earth. So God created man in his own image, in the image of God created he him; male and female created he them.

Genesis 1:26-27

And the Lord God formed man of the dust of the ground, and breathed into his nostrils the breath of life; and man became a living soul.

Genesis 2:7

Know ye that the Lord he is God: it is he that hath made us, and not we ourselves; we are his people, and the sheep of his pasture.

Psalm 100:3

The citizens of this world have been trying to live independently of God. The truth remains that we cannot do anything without our source. God can fix any health issue if only we can trust him and follow his ways. There are many factors that combine to make for healthy living. I will be introducing the different factors as the Holy Spirit enables me. Medicine and alternative medicine can provide cures but healing and wholeness comes only from God and is available to you.

I have good news for you who are reading this book. Sickness and diseases has been taken away in Christ Jesus and can be completely taken away from your body.

But he was wounded for our transgressions; he was bruised for our iniquities: the chastisement of our peace was upon him; and with his stripes we are healed.

Isaiah 53:5

Stay with me as I reveal the secret of healthy living, by simply following God's instructions, as unveiled to me by the Spirit of God, and you shall never be sick again in Jesus name.

Tony O. Akpati

November, 2019

CHAPTER ONE

THE NEED FOR SALVATION

There is no better place to begin this discussion on the subject of God's provision for health than salvation. This is because it addresses the very root cause of the problem of sickness. Sickness as well as every other calamity that has befallen humanity can be traceable to only one source and one source alone. That is man's rebellion against God. Until the redemption question is answered there can be no permanent solution to the issue of sickness.

Cutting the leaves and branches off a tree does not kill the tree. It can make the tree dormant for a while but after sometime it will sprout again. But cutting the roots of that tree will definitely kill the tree. At first it might appear as if the tree is still alive, but as long as the roots are cut, after a short time it will wither and die. Until we deal with the root of sickness once and for all, there will be no lasting solution to the endemic problem of sickness. The root cause of sickness is sin. If sickness must be eradicated or its effect minimized, we must deal with the issue of sin. Everyone born into this world is born in a state of sin.

Behold, I was shapen in iniquity; and in sin did my mother conceive me.

Psalms 51:5

"For all have sinned, and come short of the glory of God"

Romans 3:23

Remission or forgiveness of sin is the first thing that takes place in the process of salvation so that the sin which limits us is completely taken away. But that is not the end of the work of redemption. The ultimate goal of redemption is to restore man to his original state and prepare him for his final rest. That is his rightful place in God. Salvation plays a very significant role when it comes to our health. No one can access sound health without salvation.

Jesus answered and said unto him, Verily, verily, I say unto thee, Except a man be born again, he cannot see the kingdom of God. Nicodemus saith unto him, How can a man be born when he is old? can he enter the second time into his mother's womb, and be born? Jesus answered, Verily, verily, I say unto thee, Except a man be born of water and of the Spirit, he cannot enter into the kingdom of God. That which is born of the flesh is flesh; and that which is born of the Spirit is spirit. Marvel not that I said unto thee, Ye must be born again. The wind bloweth where it listeth, and thou hearest the sound thereof, but canst not tell whence it cometh, and whither it goeth: so is every one that is born of the Spirit.

John 3:3-8

What then is this salvation? First, I will tell you what it is not. Salvation is not a religious cliché, it is not a belief system, and it is not the doctrine of any church nor is it the idea of any man. Salvation or being born again is the restoration of the relationship that man had with God in the beginning which was lost in Adam through sin. It is a supernatural change in life which brings one into a covenant relationship with God, in which one allows God to influence his or her life on daily basis. Without salvation we will be stuck with the old sinful nature, the fallen human nature, and we remain enemies of God and do not have the right to access the manifold blessings of God, which includes sound health.

That at that time ye were without Christ, being aliens from the commonwealth of Israel, and strangers from the covenants of promise, having no hope, and without God in the world:

Ephesians 2:12

That's why Jesus said in the book of John chapter three in verse seven;

Marvel not that I said unto thee, Ye must be born again.

John 3:7

Salvation is not optional, if we desire God's best. It is not a suggestion either, but a direct command from the Lord Jesus. He used the word, "must" to emphasize how essentially dependent everyone's life is on salvation or being born again. Salvation enlists you as a member of God's family. This gives you the exclusive preserve to access any of the many blessings of God.

He that hath the Son hath life; and he that hath not the Son of God hath not life.

1 John 5:12

Everything in the kingdom of God begins with salvation. Salvation, otherwise known as redemption, is the most radical experience anyone can have on this side of eternity. Theology is the theory about God. One can have a sound theology and yet not have an encounter with Jesus. Salvation otherwise called redemption is an encounter with Jesus which births a new life in a person. I am strongly emphasizing salvation because it is the basic requirement to accessing all of God's provisions, sound health inclusive. Salvation makes one a child of God. It is important to mention that not everyone is a child of God. Although God created all humans, some choose not to acknowledge him.

He came to His own, and His own did not receive Him. But as many as received Him, to them He gave the right to become children of God, to those who believe in His name.

John 1:11-12 (NKJV)

No one can enjoy God's best in any area of life without being born again. Salvation is the core requirement for a relationship with God. That's why Jesus said "You must be born again" (John 3:7). In other words, you must be a bonafide member of the kingdom of God. When you understand the role of redemption in healthy living, you will appreciate the fact that medical science is not the ultimate solution to the issue of health. There is a better way to health, something beyond the medical science. Sickness and disease are intrinsic to the human fallen nature. This is because sickness was one of the curses that befell man when he disobeyed God's command.

But it shall come to pass, if thou wilt not hearken unto the voice of the Lord thy God, to observe to do all his commandments and his statutes which I command thee this day; that all these curses shall come upon thee, and overtake thee: Cursed shalt thou be in the city, and cursed shalt thou be in the field. Cursed shall be thy basket and thy store. Cursed shall be the fruit of thy body, and the fruit of thy land, the increase of thy kine, and the flocks of thy sheep.

Deuteronomy 28:15-18

But praise God! Christ has redeemed us from the curse of the law.

Christ hath redeemed us from the curse of the law, being made a curse for us: for it is written, Cursed is every one that hangeth on a tree: That the blessing of Abraham might come on the Gentiles through Jesus Christ; that we might receive the promise of the Spirit through faith.

Galatians 3:13-14

This is where the work of redemption comes into play. Through redemption there is a quickening that takes place in our spirit which impacts our bodies. The life of God originally in man that was once lost in Eden is restored back in man. There is a spiritual transaction that took place at redemption which is called regeneration.

Not by works of righteousness which we have done, but according to his mercy he saved us, by the washing of regeneration, and renewing of the Holy Ghost;

Titus 3:5

That word regeneration, spiritually speaking, implies to re-gene. The gene of God in man that Adam lost in Eden was restored to the redeemed. It is one of the remarkable things that happened to us at redemption. Practically, a new gene was infused into your DNA at salvation. This gene is dominant and it subjugates the gene of our biological parents, making them recessive. The fact that one's family history has a particular sickness does not translate that one should have that sickness if the person is born again. It is the same gene that Jesus carried during his earthly mission. Jesus was born of the Spirit and by redemption we are born of the Spirit. There was no record of Jesus being sick in the entire Bible. That's why the scripture says;

"...because as he is, so are we in this world."

1 John 4:17

Jesus also said

Then said Jesus to them again, Peace be unto you: as my Father hath sent me, even so send I you.

John 20:21

The Father sent him without any health issues or concerns, even so He sent us, to live without sickness.

One of God's most prominent desires for us is sound heath.

Beloved, I wish above all things that thou mayest prosper and be in health, even as thy soul prospereth.

3 John 1:2

There is no human fix for the problem of sin no matter the level of advancement we attain. The only fix for man's sin is the precious blood of Jesus Christ.

And almost all things are by the law purged with blood; and without shedding of blood is no remission.

Hebrews 9:22

For every child of God, God wants you to be free from the oppression of the devil. Sickness-free life is God's will for you. God is only responsible for his children. It is absolutely impossible to enjoy the blessing of sound, uninterrupted divine health if you are not a child of God. There are general blessings but there are also blessings exclusively reserved for the children of God, and sound health is one of them.

And ought not this woman, being a daughter of Abraham, whom Satan hath bound, lo, these eighteen years, be loosed from this bond on the sabbath day?

Luke 13:16

One day a woman came to Jesus desiring him to heal her sick daughter but;

He replied, "It is not right to take the children's bread and toss it to the dogs."

Matthew 15:26 (NIV)

Dogs are those that do not have relationship with Christ. They are not children of God.

But outside are dogs and sorcerers and sexually immoral and murderers and idolaters, and whoever loves and practices a lie.

Revelation 22:15 (NKJV)

Salvation is the gateway to all that God provided for humanity through Christ. It is a spiritual experience in which the Spirit of God comes to dwell in a person in the form of the Holy Spirit thereby giving the person a new birth.

Therefore if any man be in Christ, he is a new creature: old things are passed away; behold, all things are become new.

2 Corinthians 5:17

This new creature, which is the new you, is not subject to sickness. But you need to learn how to live the new life in the kingdom of God. This is where many miss it. They continue to live their old way of life even as a new creature. It will not work.

And no man putteth new wine into old bottles: else the new wine doth burst the bottles, and the wine is spilled, and the bottles will be marred: but new wine must be put into new bottles.

Mark 2:22

Those were the words of Jesus. Notice the keyword "must" again in this scripture. You must dedicate yourself to searching the scriptures to learn how to think, talk, and act as a new creature. Read anointed books from men of God of proven integrity. Being born again grants us access to hearing the voice of God. The message of the Bible will not profit anyone that is not born again. This is because the Bible is not an intellectual book but a spiritual one.

God is a Spirit: and they that worship him must worship him in spirit and in truth.

John 4:24

We can only relate to God in the spirit.

As a born again child of God, the sicknesses that were identified with your family tree cannot be traceable to you anymore. This is because your blood line has changed. You have the same blood line as Jesus. There is no cancer in his blood, there is no diabetes in his blood, there is no hypertension in his blood, and so forth. Believe it and you shall never be sick again in Jesus. Amen!

CHAPTER TWO

GOD'S WILL IS TOTAL HEALTH

Beloved, I wish above all things that thou mayest prosper and be in health, even as thy soul prospereth.

3 John 1:2

Nothing can be truer than the truth. One of the foremost priorities of God is the health of his children. God wants us to enjoy sound health. He made provision for our health, healing and wholeness in redemption. This kind of health is outside the order of this world. It is health from God not from the doctors or from the hospitals. It is health that cannot breakdown or be plagued with any form of sickness or disease. It is supernatural health.

"...I am come that they might have life, and that they might have it more abundantly."

John 10:10

Good health is God's will for us and God wants his will to be done in our lives just as it is in heaven. There is no sickness in heaven.

And he said unto them, When ye pray, say, Our Father which art in heaven, Hallowed be thy name. Thy kingdom come. Thy will be done, as in heaven, so in earth.

Luke 11:2

There is a need to emphasize that sickness and disease are not from God. God is consistent in his character. He is not responsible for anyone's affliction or sickness.

Every good gift and every perfect gift is from above, and cometh down from the Father of lights, with whom is no variableness, neither shadow of turning.

James 1:17

If ye then, being evil, know how to give good gifts unto your children, how much more shall your Father which is in heaven give good things to them that ask him?

Matthew 7:11

No sane parent will punish his or her child with sickness, no matter the gravity of their wrong doing.

For God so loved the world, that he gave his only begotten Son, that whosoever believeth in him should not perish, but have everlasting life.

John 3:16

Sickness is evil and every evil comes from the devil. Do not accept sickness in any form or shape, refuse and reject it. Do not entertain the thought that sickness is a form of trial, or punishment from God. The devil is responsible for every sickness. From the life of Job we can see clearly that it is the devil that puts sickness in people's body.

So went Satan forth from the presence of the Lord, and smote Job with sore boils from the sole of his foot unto his crown.

Job 2:7

God wants us to be healthy, whole and strong. He paid the price for us to enjoy these blessings through the death of his only begotten son Jesus Christ. Many people today do not know this truth or they don't believe it. God's heart desire for us is good health and he has paid the price for it. Sickness and disease have no right to stay in your body.

For ye are bought with a price: therefore glorify God in your body, and in your spirit, which are God's.

1 Corinthians 6:20

The devil has deprived us of this and many other blessings for too long. It is time for us to recover all lost ground. The truth is that the devil takes advantage of one's ignorance to deprive one of what rightfully belongs to him or her. When Jesus said, *"...It is finished,..."* John 19:30, he meant that the price has been fully paid for the redemption of mankind; spirit, soul and body. He did not make any payment plan neither did he make a partial payment. He paid the full price for our redemption with his own sinless blood. Unfortunately many believe the lie of the devil, that sickness is a normal part of this life. To such people, there is nothing wrong with getting sick once in a while. However, when a person receives the truth and understands it, he or she can literally drive the evil one away from his or her domain and take control of his or her health.

My people are destroyed for lack of knowledge:...

Hosea 4:6

The only cure for ignorance is knowledge. Go for the knowledge of the truth.

And ye shall know the truth, and the truth shall make you free.

John 8:32

It is not quoting the scripture but knowing the truth that makes for freedom. When this knowledge enters your heart and not just your head, you will be convinced beyond any doubt that it is God's will for you. It is only the truth of God's word that can liberate a person from the oppression of the spirit of infirmity.

If the Son therefore shall make you free, ye shall be free indeed.

John 8:36

If you can receive this truth in your heart, there is no force on earth that can put sickness in your body.

Understanding the truth is very important if one desires to enjoy the benefits of redemption. Understanding is power. The level of your understanding sets the limit of the liberty you will enjoy. Redemption does not guarantee freedom from the oppression of the devil. You cannot scare the devil by speaking in tongues when you lack knowledge. There are many redeemed children of God that are being tormented and afflicted by the devil and are victims of sicknesses and diseases. It is only your understanding of the truth that creates freedom. Understanding is the key that unlocks the treasures of redemption.

The righteousness of thy testimonies is everlasting: give me understanding, and I shall live.

Psalms 119:144

Good understanding giveth favour: but the way of transgressors is hard.

Proverbs 13:15

When Jesus explaining the parable of the sower to his disciples he said this;

But he that received seed into the good ground is he that heareth the word, and understandeth it; which also beareth fruit, and bringeth forth, some an hundredfold, some sixty, some thirty.

Matthew 13:23

When understanding is not in place, the redeemed will share the same experience with the unbeliever.

One day a leper came to Jesus, as we read in the following passage of scripture;

And, behold, there came a leper and worshipped him, saying, Lord, if thou wilt, thou canst make me clean. And Jesus put forth his hand, and touched him, saying, I will; be thou clean. And immediately his leprosy was cleansed.

Matthew 8:2-3

Notice the response of Jesus, "I will". It was spontaneous. Just like saying, that is why I came in the first place. I have been longing for you to know this all this while. You don't have to carry this sickness in your body any more. The result was instant healing. Leprosy, an incurable disease by all human standard disappeared in a split second.

"...For this purpose the Son of God was manifested, that he might destroy the works of the devil."

1 John 3:8

Jesus, the Word incarnate, came to reveal the will of the Father to us.

For I came down from heaven, not to do mine own will, but the will of him that sent me.

John 6:38

The only place you can find the will of God is in the word of God. You don't feel the will of God; it is not something you think. There is no guessing about it. It is already written in the Bible. Many are ignorant of God's provisions and they suffer not because God wants them to but because they simply lack the knowledge. Recently the U.S government offered child credit in the tax code. If you file your tax with your eligible children, and you don't know this or you fail to claim that credit, you will miss out of that benefit. The IRS (Internal Revenue Service) will not give it to you just because you don't know or that you forgot to claim it. So it is with the provisions of God. It is our responsibility to find out our inheritances in Christ and to claim those inheritances. Don't miss out of God's provisions for your health.

CHAPTER THREE

SPIRIT, SOUL AND BODY

There is need to understand the triune nature of man, that man is a spirit, he has a soul and lives in a body. It is important for us to distinguish between these three unique components of the unique creature called man.

The most valuable possession we have as humans is not a huge bank account, the jewels, the exotic cars and so on, but our bodies. Your physical body is required to maintain your physical existence here on earth. There is no human being that has a spare body. If you abuse and wear out this body, which one will you live in? You need to take good care of your body. When you take a look at a person you see only their body. The body that you see, and we each carry one about every day, is not all there is about existence as human being. Man is not just a physical entity; he has a spiritual component as well. This is an aspect of our being that is intangible yet it plays vital role in our total health. Academic knowledge does not have what it takes to unravel this dimension of our existence. It takes an understanding of the two components, the physical and the spiritual to be able to address the issue of sickness and disease effectively. Sickness and diseases have been ravaging the entire human race since the fall of man, advancement in medicine notwithstanding. It is time for us to understand what God said about our health and walk in the light of that truth in order to live a healthy life.

God conceived the design and the entire makeup of the human body. He molded the body with dirt from the ground, but the breath of his nostrils transformed the lifeless clay into living tissues that formed the intricate human body systems.

And the Lord God formed man of the dust of the ground, and breathed into his nostrils the breath of life; and man became a living soul. Genesis 2:7

How much less in them that dwell in houses of clay, whose foundation is in the dust, which are crushed before the moth?

Job 4:19

Clay vessels are very fragile, and as such, they should be handled with care.

With the body we make contact with this material world through our five senses; touch, sight, hearing, smell, and taste.

And the very God of peace sanctify you wholly; and I pray God your whole spirit and soul and body be preserved blameless unto the coming of our Lord Jesus Christ.

1 Thessalonians 5:23

The body is the house where you live. The real you is a spirit. The spirit can be alive and active towards God or dead and dormant, depending on whether one is born again or not. Your spirit needs the word of God to be healthy. What food is to our physical body, the word of God is to our spirit. The soul is the middleman between you (spirit) and your body. Inside the soul resides your mind, your will and your emotions. The soul acts just like the central processing unit (CPU) of a computer. It takes information from the body through the five sense organs, which serve as the input devices to the soul, and relays it to the spirit and vice versa. The struggle a lot of people have takes place in the soul because the information the soul gets from the spirit is not what the body is used to. Imagine saying to a person diagnosed of a terminal illness "you are not sick." He or she will find it difficult to comprehend what you are saying. This is because he or she is basing his or her judgment on the way he or she feels. I am not disproving the fact that there is severe pain and discomfort of the body. All I am simply doing is asserting the truth, you are a spirit and a spirit cannot be sick. When God was speaking in the book of Genesis chapter one;

And God said, Let us make man in our image, after our likeness: and let them have dominion over the fish of the sea, and over the fowl of the air, and over the cattle, and over all the earth, and over every creeping thing that creepeth upon the earth.

Genesis 1:26

God is saying that you, the spirit, should have dominion over your body, which is made of the dirt of the earth. The body should not dictate how we live. Don't go by how you feel. You are a spirit and the five senses do not have any access to the spirit. You cannot feel the spirit. The only way to know the spirit is by the word of God. Do you know that no one has ever seen his or her face? All we see through the mirror is a reflection of our faces. When you look into the mirror you are convinced that the image you see is really what you look like. This is because you have seen the reflection of your face over and over in the mirror. So also no one can see his or her spirit to know what the spirit looks like except through the mirror of the word of God.

But be doers of the word, and not hearers only, deceiving yourselves. For if anyone is a hearer of the word and not a doer, he is like a man observing his natural face in a mirror; for he observes himself, goes away, and immediately forgets what kind of man he was. But he who looks into the perfect law of liberty and continues in it, and is not a forgetful hearer but a doer of the work, this one will be blessed in what he does.

James 1:22-25 (NKJV)

But we all, with open face beholding as in a glass the glory of the Lord, are changed into the same image from glory to glory, even as by the Spirit of the Lord.

2 Corinthians 3:18

The more you look into the mirror of God's word, the more you understand your true identity. You are a spirit and you are not meant to be sick. If you can understand this distinction and believe it, it will go a long way to help you overcome the fear that brings sicknesses and diseases. Everyone's life moves in the direction of one's belief. What you don't believe you cannot become. Let me draw an analogy from the house, the residential home where you live. If for example that house has some electrical or plumbing problems, take for example, your bathtub is not draining properly. You don't freak out and go into panic mode because of that. The problem is with the bathtub which is a part of the house and not you, the occupant of the house. Although it might cause you some inconvenience, it does not call for worry. Man is a spirit, and a spirit cannot be sick. The human body is made of dust. Due to the fall of man the body became so porous that it has affinity for almost anything. So when you feel some symptoms or receive any diagnosis, it doesn't mean you are sick. It simply indicates that the issue is with your house and not you. The truth is that everyone feels sick at one point or another but it is not everyone that gets sick. One can only fall sick if one doesn't have this understanding. But if understanding is in place, it will take away the fear and anxiety which actually makes you feel or become sick. Each of these components of man plays a significant role in the total well-being of the total man. When a person is not born again every decision is made by the body through the five senses; sight, smell, hearing, taste, and touch. But when a person becomes born again he or she is expected to yield every right of decision making to the spirit. Interestingly, the spirit makes its decision based on the word of God.

For we walk by faith, not by sight:
                                              2 Corinthians 5:7

Until you leave the realm of feeling you cannot enjoy sound health. Many Christian believers fall back to their old ways, allowing the body to be in control. This is one of the greatest hindrances to enjoying sound health as ordained by God. When you truly understand this truth about the subject of spirit, soul and body it will help you to rightly position your mind so as not to give any room to fear any time sickness tries to attack your body. Instead you fight against it with confidence. Do not believe the lies of the devil. You are not sick and you can never be sick.

For God hath not given us the spirit of fear; but of power, and of love, and of a sound mind.

2 Timothy 1:7

You shall overcome in Jesus name.

CHAPTER FOUR

LIVING BY THE WORD

"...man doth not live by bread only, but by every word that proceedeth out of the mouth of the Lord doth man live."

Deuteronomy 8:3

My son, attend to my words; incline thine ear unto my sayings. Let them not depart from thine eyes; keep them in the midst of thine heart. For they are life unto those that find them, and health to all their flesh.

Proverbs 4:20-22

Anyone who desires the kind of health that only God can offer, health without any issues or concerns, must be willing to follow God's instructions. There is what we need to know and there is what we need to do in order to enjoy the blessings of God. The promises of scriptures place a responsibility on us in order to enjoy them. And until we play our part, God cannot be committed. For a proper and efficient use of the body we must be willing to act on the word of God the way we would act on the word of the doctor. You must believe what God said above your present reality. There is no shortcut to it. We shortchange ourselves and do ourselves a great disservice when we don't follow his instructions. To use any product outside of the manufacturer's guidelines is not a good idea even though it may seem harmless to do so. What food is to our physical body, the word of God is to our spirit. Kenneth E Hagin said many years ago that "many Christians eat three square meals a day and their spirit is malnourished". Think about that for a moment. The word of God plays a significant role in determining our total health.

Now Jacob's well was there. Jesus therefore, being wearied with his journey, sat thus on the well: and it was about the sixth hour. There cometh a woman of Samaria to draw water: Jesus saith unto her, Give me to drink. (For his disciples were gone away unto the city to buy meat.) Then saith the woman of Samaria unto him, How is it that thou, being a Jew, askest drink of me, which am a woman of Samaria? for the Jews have no dealings with the Samaritans. Jesus answered and said unto her, If thou knewest the gift of God, and who it is that saith to thee, Give me to drink; thou wouldest have asked of him, and he would have given thee living water. The woman saith unto him, Sir, thou hast nothing to draw with, and the well is deep: from whence then hast thou that living water? Art thou greater than our father Jacob, which gave us the well, and drank thereof himself, and his children, and his cattle? Jesus answered and said unto her, Whosoever drinketh of this water shall thirst again: But whosoever drinketh of the water that I shall give him shall never thirst; but the water that I shall give him shall be in him a well of water springing up into everlasting life. The woman saith unto him, Sir, give me this water, that I thirst not, neither come hither to draw.

John 4:6-15

From the above passage of scripture we can emphatically say that any solution concerning any issue of life, including health and wellness, obtained outside the word of God, at best can only produce a temporal result. The only lasting solution to any issue is the word-solution. Why do we go for that which is temporal when we can obtain a permanent solution at no cost? Yes at no cost. All it will cost you is to sit down and study your Bible, and go to where you can hear the truth of God's word being preached, which will build up your faith.

Wherefore do ye spend money for that which is not bread? and your labour for that which satisfieth not? hearken diligently unto me, and eat ye that which is good, and let your soul delight itself in fatness.

Isaiah 55:2

There is something unique about the word of God. It carries the virtues from God which makes for healings and diverse kinds of supernatural manifestations. It carries with it the very nature of God which is anti-sickness.

He sent his word, and healed them, and delivered them from their destructions.
Psalm 107:20

The level of liberty you enjoy is a function of your understanding of the word of God.

"...but the people that do know their God shall be strong, and do exploits."
Daniel 11:32

It is very pathetic that so many Christian believers cannot trust the word of God.

For my people have committed two evils; they have forsaken me the fountain of living waters, and hewed them out cisterns, broken cisterns, that can hold no water.
Jeremiah 2:13

Believers are quick to take any prescription from the doctors but not from God. We trust the words of the doctors more than the word of God. Jeremiah said,

"Thy words were found, and I did eat them; and thy word was unto me the joy and rejoicing of mine heart: for I am called by thy name, O Lord God of hosts."

Jeremiah 5:16

Constant feeding on the word of God will practically drive sickness away from your body and keep it at bay. It makes it practically impossible for sickness to have any hold on you. This is because the word of God carries medicinal properties in it.

My son, attend to my words; incline thine ear unto my sayings. Let them not depart from thine eyes; keep them in the midst of thine heart. For they are life unto those that find them, and health to all their flesh.

Proverbs 4:20-22

You need to cultivate a new habit of daily reading of God's word. Also, the word of God as water (Ephesians 5:26), flushes your entire body system as you study it. You can get off any medication if only you can trust God, believing his word and committing yourself to daily reading, studying, and meditating on the scriptures. Medications, both prescription and over the counter, can only treat symptoms and are never designed to be a permanent solution to the issue of sickness. That's why one has to keep on refilling and refilling.

Go up into Gilead, and take balm, O virgin, the daughter of Egypt: in vain shalt thou use many medicines; for thou shalt not be cured.

Jeremiah 46:11

"...let God be true, but every man a liar..."

Romans 3:4

"...by two immutable things, in which it was impossible for God to lie,"

Hebrews 6:18

God revealed Himself and his thoughts towards us all through the bible. Listen to what he said;

Beloved, I wish above all things that thou mayest prosper and be in health, even as thy soul prospereth.

3 John 1:2

God wants us whole and healthy. Anything contrary to that is a lie from the pit of hell. Do not believe the lies of the devil.

CHAPTER FIVE

THE PLACE OF FAITH

Faith is not a religious dogma that some people are fed through the teaching of some manmade religious doctrines. Genuine faith is born out of encounter with the living word of God. In order to enjoy sound health, you need this faith. Faith is the foundation upon which health and healthy living, and every other promise of the kingdom is built. You can't lay only the foundation of a building and claim that you have built a house. You will need other spiritual virtues to make your faith effective and productive.

And beside this, giving all diligence, add to your faith virtue; and to virtue knowledge; And to knowledge temperance; and to temperance patience; and to patience godliness; And to godliness brotherly kindness; and to brotherly kindness charity. For if these things be in you, and abound, they make you that ye shall neither be barren nor unfruitful in the knowledge of our Lord Jesus Christ. But he that lacketh these things is blind, and cannot see afar off, and hath forgotten that he was purged from his old sins. Wherefore the rather, brethren, give diligence to make your calling and election sure: for if ye do these things, ye shall never fall:

2 Peter 1:5-10

If you desire the kind of health we have been talking about, which is divine health, then faith is a must. Faith is a formidable weapon in the hand of the believer. With faith you can subdue any sickness no matter what name it is called. It is faith that makes one believe what the Bible says, even when it seems irrational from the human perspective.

And what shall I more say? for the time would fail me to tell of Gedeon, and of Barak, and of Samson, and of Jephthae; of David also, and Samuel, and of the prophets: Who through faith subdued kingdoms, wrought righteousness, obtained promises, stopped the mouths of lions. Quenched the violence of fire, escaped the edge of the sword, out of weakness were made strong, waxed valiant in fight, turned to flight the armies of the aliens.

Hebrews 11:32-34

By faith you can overcome sickness.

For whatsoever is born of God overcometh the world: and this is the victory that overcometh the world, even our faith.

1 John 5:4

It is possible to enjoy a sickness-free life, without any issues or concerns, all by faith.

Jesus said unto him, If thou canst believe, all things are possible to him that believeth.

Mark 9:23

Faith is not just believing but acting on God's word to prove that you believe him.

But wilt thou know, O vain man, that faith without works is dead?

James 2:20

FIGHT FOR YOUR HEALTH

And from the days of John the Baptist until now the kingdom of heaven suffereth violence, and the violent take it by force.

Matthew 11:12

With your faith you fight to retain your health. This has nothing to do with physical exertion of force as in conflict. The Bible calls it the fight of faith and it is a good fight.

….Fight the good fight of faith.

1 Timothy 6:12

Anyone that refuses to fight will end up a victim of sickness and diseases. This is because the Bible says;

The just shall live by his faith.

Habakkuk 4:2

Sicknesses and diseases have their root in the spiritual realm. What we see and know as sicknesses and diseases are more spiritual than they are physical. A spiritual approach is the only way to deal with it. Anything short of that will make sound health an illusion. Make no mistake about it, no doctor or hospital can guarantee sound health. I guarantee you that. Even your doctors have doctors they go to see. There is a better way, and that is the way of God. His ways are superior to any technological breakthrough in medicine ever known to man. God is not in the same class with man. Many times we tend to match God with man. Man is no match for God.

For my thoughts are not your thoughts, neither are your ways my ways, saith the Lord. For as the heavens are higher than the earth, so are my ways higher than your ways, and my thoughts than your thoughts.

Isaiah 55:8-9

Ironically, his ways are not complex. As a matter of fact, his ways are so simple that we find it difficult to believe, and it costs nothing monetarily. Imagine for a moment living the rest of your life without any health concerns. It is possible.

But I fear, lest by any means, as the serpent beguiled Eve through his subtilty, so your minds should be corrupted from the simplicity that is in Christ.

2 Corinthians 11:3

Hey! It is possible and it is available if only you can believe.

Jesus said unto him, If thou canst believe, all things are possible to him that believeth.

Mark 9:23

There are tons of people that are living in the sickness-free zone all by faith. Faith is very crucial to how healthy we are. That's why it is critical that we invest in the subject of faith in order to take delivery of our health inheritance. When your faith comes alive you begin to live as if sickness does not exist.

For we wrestle not against flesh and blood, but against principalities, against powers, against the rulers of the darkness of this world, against spiritual wickedness in high places.

Ephesians 6:12

It does not matter where you live on the face of the earth, whether in a developed country or a third world country as they call it, your placement in the spectrum of wealth does not matter, whether you are rich or poor, everyone is vulnerable to the attack of one form of sickness or another. The devil, who comes *to steal, to kill, and to destroy* is the architect – John 10:10. There is not one person that is exempted. However there are varying outcomes, depending on one's position in God. It is only *"those that do know their God"* that can overcome the enemy – Daniel 11:32

Jesus gave a classic illustration of the importance of faith in the word of God in the book of Matthew chapter seven beginning from verse twenty-four, he said:

Therefore whosoever heareth these sayings of mine, and doeth them, I will liken him unto a wise man, which built his house upon a rock: And the rain descended, and the floods came, and the winds blew, and beat upon that house; and it fell not: for it was founded upon a rock. And every one that heareth these sayings of mine, and doeth them not, shall be likened unto a foolish man, which built his house upon the sand: And the rain descended, and the floods came, and the winds blew, and beat upon that house; and it fell: and great was the fall of it.

Matthew 7:24-27

The same weather conditions; rain, flood, and wind descended on both buildings but they each had different outcomes. This speaks of two categories of people, based on their attitude towards the word of God. While one received the word with its attendant responsibilities the other cares less.

Faith is a must if you want to enjoy sound health. Your faith in God is a deterrent to the assault of sickness and disease. It keeps them at bay. It makes you a "touch not" entity.

When they went from one nation to another, from one kingdom to another people; He suffered no man to do them wrong: yea, he reproved kings for their sakes; Saying, Touch not mine anointed, and do my prophets no harm.

Psalm 105:13-15

It takes the fight of faith to receive your portion of what Christ has made available for us through redemption. Until you stand up for your rights in redemption sound health will be an illusion.

Rise ye up, take your journey, and pass over the river Arnon: behold, I have given into thine hand Sihon the Amorite, king of Heshbon, and his land: begin to possess it, and contend with him in battle.

Deuteronomy 2:24

It is not enough to be born again; you must know your responsibilities, your rights and privileges in Christ. You must know what belongs to you in Christ. Bishop David O. Oyedepo said, "Any faith that makes God absolutely responsible for the outcome of our lives is an irresponsible faith." We have a role to play if we desire to live healthy.

My people are destroyed for lack of knowledge

Hosea 4:6a

What you don't know gives the devil advantage over you but what you know makes you rule over him and keep him away from your territory.

ENGAGING IN THE FIGHT

Sickness is a spirit and as such it is invisible. What we see and know as sicknesses today, from medical diagnosis to laboratory results are the symptoms or the manifestation of the activities of that spirit. The Bible calls it the spirit of infirmity:

And, behold, there was a woman which had a spirit of infirmity eighteen years, and was bowed together, and could in no wise lift up herself Luke 13:11

The best way to deal with sickness is to go to its roots by dealing with the spirit that sponsors them. The question becomes, how do you fight something invisible? Jesus said in the book of John chapter six verse sixty-three,

"It is the spirit that quickeneth; the flesh profiteth nothing: the words that I speak unto you, they are spirit, and they are life.

When you receive the word, the Spirit of God enters you.

And the spirit entered into me when he spake unto me, and set me upon my feet, that I heard him that spake unto me.

Ezekiel 2:2

When you speak the Word you release the Spirit of God and the Spirit of God deals with the spirit of infirmity to destroy it. Speaking the Word of God helps you to overcome sicknesses and other vices that want to dominate one's life and make one a captive. Science has confirmed that every word we speak is transmitted through our nerves. So, when you speak the word of God you are speaking life and health into your body.

The centurion answered and said, Lord, I am not worthy that thou shouldest come under my roof: but speak the word only, and my servant shall be healed.

Matthew 8:8

Say only what the word of God said concerning you, not how you feel. This is a spiritual law. Just as we have natural laws, like the law of gravity, so also we have spiritual laws.

And the inhabitant shall not say, I am sick: the people that dwell therein shall be forgiven their iniquity.

Isaiah 33:24

This is a spiritual law. Do not let it come out from your mouth, that you are sick. It doesn't matter how you feel, do not say I am sick, or I have this or that. There are so many people that are religious but they don't live by faith and they don't observe any spiritual laws. Such people will poison your faith with their unbelief. I call them unbelieving believers.

HOW DO I GROW MY FAITH

If faith is that important, how then can one grow his or her faith?

So then faith cometh by hearing, and hearing by the word of God.

Romans 10:17

Constant hearing of God's word is the major way to grow your faith. Nothing happens by chance. It is very important that we constantly invest in the subject of faith because without it we will be plagued by sickness and disease. Faith is a deterrent to the devil. It is the currency used for every spiritual transaction. Faith does not deny the existence of reality or facts, but faith is superior to both.

Jesus said unto him, If thou canst believe, all things are possible to him that believeth.

Mark 9:23

Growing up as a young believer, the Holy Spirit opened my eyes to the need for spiritual growth by painting a scriptural picture with these scriptures;

Now ye are the body of Christ, and members in particular.

1 Corinthians 12:27

For the husband is the head of the wife, even as Christ is the head of the church: and he is the saviour of the body.

Ephesians 5:23

And I will put enmity between thee and the woman, and between thy seed and her seed; it shall bruise thy head, and thou shalt bruise his heel.

Genesis 3:15

For unto us a child is born, unto us a son is given: and the government shall be upon his shoulder: and his name shall be called Wonderful, Counselor, The mighty God, The everlasting Father, The Prince of Peace.

Isaiah 9:6

"...no man can say that Jesus is the Lord, but by the Holy Ghost".

1 Corinthians 12:3

From the above scriptures and relating them with the human body, Christ is the head. The Holy Ghost as the neck links the head to the body, for there is no connection between the body and the head without the neck. From the shoulders to the heels is the body. Anyone that refuses to grow remains at the heel level. Satan is permitted to assault those at that level. You have no right to complain if you are at this level. All you need to do is to take responsibility for your personal growth in the faith. It is not a church thing but a personal thing. It is not how long one has been a Christian but how committed you are to obeying his commandments. God does not place a limit on anyone's growth and development as a child of God. We are our own limit. Our location or placement in the body is not God-determined. It is a function of our personal commitment to our walk with God. The government, which speaks of authority, will be exercised by only those at the shoulder level. They are the ones that can refuse whatever the devil is offering. It takes maturity in the word of faith to refuse certain things.

By faith Moses, when he was come to years, refused to be called the son of Pharaoh's daughter;

Hebrews 11:24

Spiritual growth is not an automatic process that happens once you are born again. There is no magic in the kingdom of God. Many believers have done close to nothing with respect to the subject of spiritual growth. They don't study their Bibles neither do they read books. Faith is a must if one desires to enjoy sound health. It has no substitute. The level of liberty you enjoy is a function of your faith. In other words, your health is directly proportional to your faith. That's why Jesus will always say;

"...According to your faith be it unto you." Matthew 9:29

Another scripture says;

Above all, taking the shield of faith, wherewith ye shall be able to quench all the fiery darts of the wicked.

Ephesians 6:16

If the darts of sickness are hitting you it means that your faith shield is not wide enough. All you need do is to grow your faith.

FAITH AND MEDICATION

There is no provision for collective faith. Faith is a product of personal adventure. It operates strictly on an individual basis.

The just shall live by his faith, says the scriptures (Romans 1:17, Habakkuk 2:4, Hebrews 10:38, Galatians 3:11). As Jesus will always say;

"... According to your faith be it unto you."

Matthew 9:29

As you feed on the word of God you grow by it and your level keeps changing as you continue.

So then faith cometh by hearing, and hearing by the word of God.

Romans 10:17

Just like newborn baby graduates from milk formula to cereal and then to solid food, the same is applicable to the walk of faith. Spiritual growth otherwise called growing in faith is in stages. That you have faith today is not a guarantee that it will be there tomorrow if you do nothing about your faith. The key to success in anything we do in this kingdom is continuity and consistency.

As newborn babes, desire the sincere milk of the word, that ye may grow thereby

1 Peter 2:2

There is no magic in God's kingdom neither is there any software for faith. To acquire faith, you must be intentional about it. Let's be practical about this. Instead of surfing the internet, or listening to news or watching your favorite sports or television shows, you can invest that time in studying the Bible, reading anointed book or in listening to faith building messages. It is worth noting that faith is in levels and also, not everyone has faith. Jesus asked his disciples;

"...how is it that ye have no faith?"

Mark 4:40

At another time he said unto them

"...O ye of little faith".

Matthew 6:30

And yet to some people he said,

"... great is thy faith..."

Matthew 15:28

There are people that say that they don't take medication. You can hear them make statements such as, "In our church we don't take medication". This is not because they operate by faith but merely by their church doctrines and traditions handed down to them, which are not rooted in the Word of God. This is an assertion they make, not because they have grown their own faith but simply because it is a doctrine in their church. Such a belief system is misleading and dangerous. Such persons will die for free. The body of Christ is not divided but there are categories of believers. Taking medication is not a sin nor is it a sign that you have no faith. We are dealing with a vicious enemy on a rampage who constantly wants to assault us and afflict our bodies with sicknesses. Sometimes the attack on one's health is so severe and overwhelming that, based on one's faith level he or she might need the aid of medication for the body to recover. Just as a person who fell down might need a helping hand to get up.

For a just man falleth seven times, and riseth up again: but the wicked shall fall into mischief

Proverbs 24:16

As soon as your body recovers and as you begin to build your faith, get off the medication. Sometimes you don't need to complete the prescribed dosage. Get off of medication as quickly as you can and increase your intake of the word of God. Medication is addictive and has many side effects. It conditions the body to be dependent on it. The word of God remains our greatest asset in fighting against the assault of the enemy. It is the word of God that makes for complete healing and wholeness. Read your Bible every day.

Go up to Gilead and take balm, O virgin, the daughter of Egypt; In vain you will use many medicines; You shall not be cured.

Jeremiah 46:11

The beauty of it all is that God is working on us until we come to the unity of faith.

CHAPTER SIX

STAY AWAY FROM SIN

How much less in them that dwell in houses of clay, whose foundation is in the dust, which are crushed before the moth?

Job 4:19

The human body is a house of clay. Living in a house of clay calls for caution in the way we live. One of the greatest impediments to living in sound health as God intended is a sinful lifestyle. Sinful lifestyle is destructive. Sound health and sin are like gasoline and fire, they are incompatible. They don't go together. It is not so much about the viruses and germs in our environment that make for all these allergies, sicknesses and diseases. Although they play a part, the main cause of sickness is man's rebellion, and disobedience to God's instruction.

Hast thou not procured this unto thyself, in that thou hast forsaken the Lord thy God, when he led thee by the way?

Jeremiah 2:17

One of the consequences of disobeying God's instructions as outlined in the scriptures is bodily afflictions in the form or sicknesses and diseases. This is evidently clear when we take a close look at the account of God's relationship with the children of Israel, as seen in the book of Deuteronomy chapter twenty-eight from verse fifteen to the end of the chapter. The words in those passages were pronouncement of curse as a result of disobedience, and sickness and diseases was one of them.

It is enough of a problem that we were all born with the sinful nature, yet some people indulge in certain outrageous behaviors that further complicate the issues. All sin can cause sickness but not all sickness is as a result of sin. For anyone to enjoy the blessing of sound health, he or she must be willing to stay away from a lifestyle of sin. God will not give anyone sound health just for the person to live any way he or she wants. The ultimate goal of a life of good health is to bring glory to God. It is of no good to bestow the blessing of good health upon anyone that will not glorify God.

We know that whoever is born of God does not sin; but he who has been born of God keeps himself, and the wicked one does not touch him.

1 John 5:18 (NKJV)

When a person is living in sin, the enemy has direct access into his or her body to afflict him or her. A life of sin is an open invitation for the assault of the enemy.

"...and whoso breaketh an hedge, a serpent shall bite him".

Ecclesiastes 10:8

Simply put, sin is anything we do, say or imagine that violates God's law. You must make every effort to stay away from sin.

If iniquity be in thine hand, put it far away, and let not wickedness dwell in thy tabernacles.

Job 11:14

In other words, eliminate sin from your life. It was sin that brought sickness in the first place. To avoid sickness, you must avoid sin. Every act of sin impacts both your physical and spiritual wellbeing. There is nothing that snuffs out the life and health in a person like sin, especially the sin of immorality. It tears down the very fabrics of our being. The word of God makes it clear in the following passage.

Flee fornication. Every sin that a man doeth is without the body; but he that committeth fornication sinneth against his own body. What? know ye not that your body is the temple of the Holy Ghost which is in you, which ye have of God, and ye are not your own?

1 Corinthians 6:18-19

Anyone living a life of sin cannot enjoy good health. There was a story in the Bible about a man who was sick for thirty-eight years. One day Jesus healed this man that had been sick for that long. This story can be found in the book of John chapter five. Jesus said to him in verse fourteen:

"...Behold, thou art made whole: sin no more, lest a worse thing come unto thee."

John 5:14

Our conflict with sin is a lifelong conflict. But we must constantly refuse sin in any form in its totality.

Be not wise in thine own eyes: fear the Lord, and depart from evil. It shall be health to thy navel, and marrow to thy bones.

Proverbs 3:7-8

Unabated life of sin will make one a victim of sickness and disease but your departure from sin is the security of your health and vitality. Sin will open the door to affliction of sickness any time. Beware of sin because sin kills.

CHAPTER SEVEN

DEAL WITH TOXIC EMOTIONS

There are different and varying emotions that we display as mankind. These emotions play significant roles in our health. Essentially, emotions are like a control device that regulates our health. Your emotional health directly impacts your physical health. In fact you are as healthy as your emotions are. It is not possible for one to be an emotional wreck and live a super healthy life. Emotional dysfunction is at the root of many sicknesses. This is because these emotions impair the normal functioning of some of the vital internal body systems responsible for automatic body processes like heart rate, digestion, metabolic process, and so on. It leads to hormonal imbalance. I do not want to sound too anatomical, that is not my goal. You can always consult your anatomy textbooks to read up on these systems. One of the dangers of these emotions is that their presence in the body cannot be readily detected with any diagnostic equipment. To take control of your health you must first take control of your emotions. Read the following passage of scripture with me;

He that hath no rule over his own spirit is like a city that is broken down, and without walls.

Proverbs 25:28

When you cannot control your emotions, you open up yourself to all manner of attack of sicknesses and diseases. There are healthy and non-healthy emotions. The non-healthy emotions are toxic and they hurt us in many ways especially in our health. The natural inclination of all humans leans more toward the non-healthy emotions. It will take a deliberate effort and a willingness to move towards the healthy emotions. Many people are emotionally sick which translates to physical sickness. Anti-depressants cannot treat emotional sickness. It may attempt to suppress the symptoms but it does not have what it takes to treat emotional sickness. It cannot get to the root of the problem. Medications are designed to treat symptoms not the actual sickness. That is why you see so many people taking anti-depressants, getting refill after refill for years and still they suffer from the same sickness. If that is your case, you can completely be set free by simply turning to God and dealing with any of these toxic emotions in your life. These emotions are the little foxes that destroy the vines and need to be taken away from our lives.

Take us the foxes, the little foxes that spoil the vines: for our vines have tender grapes.

Songs of Solomon 2:15

The lists are not exhaustive.

Worry and Anxiety:

Worry and anxiety can cause heart palpitation and psychological disorder. It is natural to encounter worrying or anxiety-provoking situations as one goes through this life. Sometimes those situations can be overwhelming. It is legitimate to show concern in the affairs of one's life. However, we should not allow them to drive us to the extreme where they become the controlling factors in all that we do.

One day Abraham was overwhelmed with the thought that he would die without having a child that will inherit him and he was old. He did not keep this worry to himself; he presented that source of worry to God in prayer.

And Abram said, Lord God, what wilt thou give me, seeing I go childless, and the steward of my house is this Eliezer of

Damascus? And Abram said, Behold, to me thou hast given no seed: and, lo, one born in my house is mine heir.

Genesis 15:2-3

God reassured him that he will not die without having his own child that will inherit him, his old age notwithstanding. On that certain night God took Abraham outside and asked him to take a look at the dark sky filled with stars and asked him to count the stars. I believe Abraham tried to count the stars but they were too numerous to count, and God said to him,

"...So shall thy seed be."

Genesis 15:4-5

That one word from God was all that Abraham needed to terminate life-long worries on the issue of barrenness.

"Therefore I say to you, do not worry about your life, what you will eat or what you will drink; nor about your body, what you will put on. Is not life more than food and the body more than clothing? Look at the birds of the air, for they neither sow nor reap nor gather into barns; yet your heavenly Father feeds them. Are you not of more value than they? Which of you by worrying can add one cubit to his stature? "So why do you worry about clothing? Consider the lilies of the field, how they grow: they neither toil nor spin; and yet I say to you that even

Solomon in all his glory was not arrayed like one of these. Now if God so clothes the grass of the field, which today is, and tomorrow is thrown into the oven, will He not much more clothe you, O you of little faith? "Therefore do not worry, saying, 'What shall we eat?' or 'What shall we drink?' or 'What shall we wear?' For after all these things the Gentiles seek. For your heavenly Father knows that you need all these things. But seek first the kingdom of God and His righteousness, and all these things shall be added to you.

Matthew 6:25-33 (NKJV)

Worry and anxiety are forms of affliction of the mind. God's wisdom to overcome worries and anxieties is to present the issues of concern to him in prayers.

Is any among you afflicted? let him pray. Is any merry? let him sing psalms.

James 5:13

Another scripture says;

Be careful for nothing; but in everything by prayer and supplication with thanksgiving let your requests be made known unto God.

Philippians 4:6

Worrying over anything does not solve the problem nor does it change anything. Instead it makes the matter worse. Worrying is like adding a problem to an already existing one. So, my question to you is, why do you worry?

Anger:

Be ye angry, and sin not: let not the sun go down upon your wrath:

Ephesians 4:26

God did not say do not be angry. He is the one that made us and he understands our nature.

For he knoweth our frame; he remembereth that we are dust.

Psalm 103:14

It is human to be angry. But it becomes a problem and a concern when one allows the anger to dominate and control one's life. God gave us the capacity to control anger.

In the book of Genesis chapter four, Cain was angry with his brother Abel because his brother's offering was accepted by God while his was not. God warned him of his anger in the following verses;

And the Lord said unto Cain, Why art thou wroth? and why is thy countenance fallen? If thou doest well, shalt thou not be accepted? and if thou doest not well, sin lieth at the door. And unto thee shall be his desire, and thou shalt rule over him.

Genesis 4:6-7

God was practically telling him to take control of his anger but he wouldn't listen. He ended up killing his brother. Anger can cause irregular heartbeat and a spike in blood pressure. There are people that have so much anger bottled up inside that they vent like the plume of fumes from a volcano. They live on the edge at all times and are ready to snap at the slightest provocation.

For the wrath of man worketh not the righteousness of God.

James 1:20

In other words anger does not produce anything good. There is no benefit or reward for being angry. It is human to be angry but don't stay angry. You can choose to be like your father God. Look at what the Bible says about him;

For his anger endureth but a moment; in his favour is life: weeping may endure for a night, but joy cometh in the morning.

Psalm 30:5

Anger becomes a sin which can lead to ill health when you stay angry for a long time. That's why we have that timely encouragement from the Bible:

Be ye angry, and sin not: let not the sun go down upon your wrath:

Ephesians 4:26

It is legitimate to be angry but it is illegitimate to stay angry. The more you hold on to anger the more vulnerable you become to the assault of sicknesses and diseases. Jesus said that it is impossible to avoid things that will make you angry.

Woe to the world because of offenses! For offenses must come, but woe to that man by whom the offense comes!

Matthew 18:7

This is a heads up, that things that will make us angry are bound to happen. Wisdom demands that we prepare our minds to deal with whatever issue that comes our way so as not to stay angry when they happen. Everyone has the propensity to be angry and stay angry. So, it is a choice to stay angry or not to stay angry. Make your choice. God will always encourage us to terminate anger in our lives. Do not let anger continue anymore in your life.

But now ye also put off all these; anger, wrath, malice, blasphemy, filthy communication out of your mouth.

Colossians 3:8

Unforgiveness:

Do not keep record of wrongs done to you. It does not matter how much pain it caused you. Learn to forgive people their offenses. Unforgiveness is a killer emotion. Many undiagnosed sicknesses can be traceable to unforgiveness. Anyone that harbors unforgiveness cannot enjoy sound health. Not forgiving others of their offense is a terrible sin. It is harmful to one's health. It is the only sin that makes God recalls our own very sin against him. God does not take it kindly when we don't forgive people their sins against us. It is a sin that gives demons the full right to torment a person with all manner of sicknesses and afflictions. Anyone that is sick but fails to forgive those that offended him or her cannot recover from that sickness if he or she insists on holding unto the offense of others against him. Living in unforgiveness is dying without knowing. There is no reason under heaven tenable before God why one should hold to unforgiveness. There is an account in the book of Matthew chapter eighteen beginning from verse fifteen where Jesus was teaching on forgiveness. The following is the discuss from that passage;

Then came Peter to him, and said, Lord, how oft shall my brother sin against me, and I forgive him? till seven times? Jesus saith unto him, I say not unto thee, Until seven times: but, Until seventy times seven. Therefore is the kingdom of heaven likened unto a certain king, which would take account of his servants. And when he had begun to reckon, one was brought unto him, which owed him ten thousand talents. But forasmuch as he had not to pay, his lord commanded him to be sold, and his wife, and children, and all that he had, and payment to be made. The servant therefore fell down, and worshipped him, saying, Lord, have patience with me, and I will pay thee all. Then the lord of that servant was moved with compassion, and loosed him, and forgave him the debt. But the same servant went out, and found one of his fellowservants, which owed him an hundred pence: and he laid hands on him, and took him by the throat, saying, Pay me that thou owest. And his fellowservant fell down at his feet, and besought him, saying, Have patience with me, and I will pay thee all. And he would not: but went and cast him into prison, till he should pay the debt. So when his fellowservants saw what was done, they were very sorry, and came and told unto their lord all that was done. Then his lord, after that he had called him, said unto him, O thou wicked servant, I forgave thee all that debt, because thou desiredst me: Shouldest not thou also have had compassion on thy fellowservant, even as I had pity on thee? And his lord was wroth, and delivered him to the tormentors, till he should pay all that was due unto him. So likewise shall my heavenly Father do also unto you, if ye from your hearts forgive not everyone his brother their trespasses.

Matthew 18:21-35

Forgive others and let God avenge you.

Dearly beloved, avenge not yourselves, but rather give place unto wrath: for it is written, Vengeance is mine; I will repay, saith the Lord.

Romans 12:19

Fear:

Fear is a negative emotion. Fear has torment, the scripture says;

There is no fear in love; but perfect love casteth out fear: because fear hath torment. He that feareth is not made perfect in love.

1 John 4:18

Fear puts people in bondage. In most cases of death it is fear that kills its victims and not the sickness.

Forasmuch then as the children are partakers of flesh and blood, he also himself likewise took part of the same; that through death he might destroy him that had the power of death, that is, the devil; And deliver them who through fear of death were all their lifetime subject to bondage.

Hebrews 2:14-15

Fear is of the devil.

For God hath not given us the spirit of fear; but of power, and of love, and of a sound mind.

2 Timothy 1:7

One dangerous thing about fear is that it attracts whatever you are fearful of. If you are afraid of heart attack, then one is on its way. Hear what Job said:

For the thing which I greatly feared is come upon me, and that which I was afraid of is come unto me.

Job 3:25

You must deal with fear and eliminate it from your life. Whatever phobia it is called, there is a spirit behind it and it is the spirit of fear from the devil. The truth is that the enemy wants to have access into our lives and he can use anything to open up a door of access.

Neither give place to the devil.

Ephesians 4:27

Don't give him any room to operate in your life. If you give the devil a foothold he will turn it to a stronghold. Instead of focusing on a negative thought, engage your mind to think about something positive. It takes one thought to displace the other. The thought of God which is the Word of God is superior to any human thought and can displace such thoughts especially when those thoughts are negative.

Hatred

A hater is a murderer, and no murderer has eternal life.

Whosoever hateth his brother is a murderer: and ye know that no murderer hath eternal life abiding in him.

1 John 3:15

Divine health is a tiny piece of eternal life. A hater is not permitted to taste of it. Consciously replace hate with love. If the devil is giving you a reason or tries to justify why you should harbor hatred in your heart, there is a cure for it. Pray for the person with all your heart. This singular act will replace hatred with love. It is a spiritual law. Jesus said;

But I say unto you, Love your enemies, bless them that curse you, do good to them that hate you, and pray for them which despitefully use you, and persecute you;

Matthew 5:44

Essentially, loving your enemies and praying for them is not for them to repent and treat you fairly but for you to be free from the evil seed of hatred. Replace hatred in your heart with the love of God. The only way we can validate our love for God is by loving other people.

If someone says, "I love God," and hates his brother, he is a liar; for he who does not love his brother whom he has seen, how can he love God whom he has not seen?

1 John 4:20 (NKJV)

You have to go out of your way to demonstrate the love of God.

Bitterness:
You can't be bitter and expect to live a better life. Bitterness grows out of untreated hurt and anger. When someone hurts you, don't pretend that everything is okay while you are angry with the person. That kind of attitude will make bitterness take root in your heart.

Looking diligently lest any man fail of the grace of God; lest any root of bitterness springing up trouble you, and thereby many be defiled;

Hebrews 12:15

Once bitterness takes root in any heart it can bring trouble of any kind and sickness is likely one of them. Do everything you can not to give the enemy the chance to plant bitterness in your heart. Listen to what the Apostle Paul said;

And herein do I exercise myself, to have always a conscience void to offence toward God, and toward men.

Acts 24:16

It takes constant exercising of one's heart for bitterness not to take root. As long as there are humans on the earth we are prone to offense. We can choose not to be embittered regardless of what has been done to us in the past.

CHAPTER EIGHT

THE GATEWAY OF THE MIND

You need a sound mind in order to enjoy sound health. The condition of your heart, thoughts, imaginations, memory, and mind directly impact your health. The mind is very strategic if one desires to enjoy good health.

Watch the traffic that is going on in your mind. Your mind is the gateway to your life. Keep a proactive surveillance over your mind. Do not allow any evil thought of sickness or any other evil thought into your mind, they are poison to the body.

Someone once said; "the heart of the matter is a matter of the heart." The place of the mind is very critical if one will enjoy sound health. Listen to what God said about our minds;

But without thy mind would I do nothing; that thy benefit should not be as it were of necessity, but willingly.

Philemon 1:14

So, the devil will have no say when the guards of our minds are up. Do you know that you can lock a person out and deny him or her access to your house? In the same way, you can lock out evil thought. The key is with you, go ahead and use it.

The mind is like a control valve to your health. Battles of life are fought, won or lost in the mind. To win the battles against sickness you must be willing to change your mind set. You are as healthy as your mind. Sickness is not an irreversible reaction. You were not born with it. It will go the same way it came. It all depends on how you think. The same blood of Jesus that saved us from sin is the blood that took away our sicknesses.

But He was wounded for our transgressions, He was bruised for our iniquities; The chastisement for our peace was upon Him, And by His stripes we are healed.

Isaiah 53:5 (NKJV)

The mind plays a significant role in the overall health of a person. There is a direct correlation between one's state of mind and his or her state of health. If you don't have a healthy mind you can't have a healthy body.

For as he thinks in his heart, so is he....

Proverbs 23:7

Our natural mind does not see things from God's perspective. As a matter of fact it does not have the capacity to do so.

But the natural man does not receive the things of the Spirit of God, for they are foolishness to him; nor can he know them, because they are spiritually discerned.

1 Corinthians 2:14

From the scriptures we can distinguish four different kinds of mind; evil mind, corrupt mind, reprobate mind and sound mind. Only the sound mind is capable of following God's instructions. That is why we are encouraged from the word of God, to renew our mind.

And be not conformed to this world: but be ye transformed by the renewing of your mind, that ye may prove what is that good, and acceptable, and perfect, will of God.

Romans 12:2

That means, the mind needs to be trained by the Word of God. The mind is used to its old way of reasoning, making its decision based on the five sense organs. The Bible has the power to change how you view life. Until the mind is renewed it cannot see things from Gods perspective. It is only when you renew your mind with the Word of God that you can understand that God wants you to be healthy and has made provision for that. To renew your mind you have to constantly and consistently obey the instructions of the Bible. Obeying God's command is more important than anything else you might want to do for God. You must yield every inch of your life to the control of the Holy Spirit.

And Samuel said, Hath the Lord as great delight in burnt offerings and sacrifices, as in obeying the voice of the Lord? Behold, to obey is better than sacrifice, and to hearken than the fat of rams.   1 Samuel 15:22

When the mind is renewed only then you will believe, and the promises of the scriptures become your practical experience.

Keep thy heart with all diligence; for out of it are the issues of life

                                       Proverbs 4:23

Stand guard at the door of your mind. Do not let in any negative thought. Vehemently refuse the thought of sickness.

Submit yourselves therefore to God. Resist the devil, and he will flee from you.   James 4:7

Resist the sickness and it will flee and look for another place to stay. You resist by telling that sickness that there is no place for it in your body. Let it know that you are the temple of the Holy Spirit and that no sickness is allowed in your body. Do not give it any place in your mind. It does not matter the kind and the degree of the physical evidence you are experiencing in your health, if your mind refuse to be convinced to accept that verdict, you cannot be sick. To be able to do that you must constantly feed your mind with the truth of God's Word. Your mind is like a fortress where you stockpile your spiritual amour, which is the Word of God. The mind works like the memory in the computer, what you feed into it is what you get out of it. Don't let it be idle for a moment. The devil and the hordes of hell constantly attack the mind with the intent to sow their evil seed, sickness being one of them. It takes one thought to displace another. That's why we need the thought of God which is his Word.

"For My thoughts are not your thoughts, Nor are your ways My ways," says the Lord. "For as the heavens are higher than the earth, So are My ways higher than your ways, And My thoughts than your thoughts.

Isaiah 55:8-9

God expects us to control our minds.

He that hath no rule over his own spirit is like a city that is broken down, and without walls.

Proverbs 25:28

Do not clutter your mind with irrelevant issues. Your life is more important than anything else. Saturate your mind with the word of God.

CHAPTER NINE

THE NEED FOR SPIRITUALITY

The way things operate in the kingdom of God is different from what is obtained in the kingdom of this world.

For my thoughts are not your thoughts, neither are your ways my ways, saith the Lord. For as the heavens are higher than the earth, so are my ways higher than your ways, and my thoughts than your thoughts.

Isaiah 55:8-9

God's way is superior to the ways of man. For us to be able to receive from God we must be spiritual. This is because;

God is a Spirit: and they that worship him must worship him in spirit and in truth.

John 4:24

We cannot relate with God outside of his Word. The Word of God is spirit (John 6:63); it is not an intellectual book. It is a spiritual book. To be spiritual is simply to view every issue of life from the lenses of the scripture.

But the natural man receiveth not the things of the Spirit of God: for they are foolishness unto him: neither can he know them, because they are spiritually discerned.

1 Corinthians 2:14

The Word of God which created the entire universe has the potential to accomplish anything. However, it will get nothing done if you don't put it to work. We need to align our thoughts and our words with the Word of God.

What man is he that desireth life, and loveth many days, that he may see good? Keep thy tongue from evil, and thy lips from speaking guile

Psalm 34:12-13

The words we speak go a long way in determining how healthy we live. It may sound silly from the world's perspective, but that's the way things work in the kingdom of God. It is a spiritual law and it is an indispensable key to your living in sound health. When you saturate your heart with the Word of God it will naturally flow from the words you speak.

O generation of vipers, how can ye, being evil, speak good things? for out of the abundance of the heart the mouth speaketh.

Matthew 12:34

God responds to the words we speak according to the contents of the words.

Say unto them, As truly as I live, saith the Lord, as ye have spoken in mine ears, so will I do to you:

Numbers 14:28

That is why God commanded in the book of Isaiah chapter thirty-three in verse twenty-four;

And the inhabitant shall not say, I am sick: the people that dwell therein shall be forgiven their iniquity.

Isaiah 33:24

You can hear some people make such statements like, "I can't be sick". That is not being boastful or arrogant as some might think. That person is just observing the spiritual law of words.

Death and life are in the power of the tongue: and they that love it shall eat the fruit thereof.

Proverbs 18:21

For verily I say unto you, That whosoever shall say unto this mountain, Be thou removed, and be thou cast into the sea; and shall not doubt in his heart, but shall believe that those things which he saith shall come to pass; he shall have whatsoever he saith.

Matthew 11:23

Faith is expressed through the words we speak, and backed by our actions. The Word of God is the raw material for creating our expectations. If you can't say it you won't experience it.

We having the same spirit of faith, according as it is written, I believed, and therefore have I spoken; we also believe, and therefore speak;

2 Corinthians 4:13

Declare boldly and make it public, the blessing of sound health God has blessed you with. Never speak about yourself based on how you feel in your body. Let the words you speak be based on the Word of God.

The centurion answered and said, Lord, I am not worthy that thou shouldest come under my roof: but speak the word only, and my servant shall be healed.

Matthew 8:8

When you speak the Word you are speaking God's perspective. And because God's Word is creative in nature, as you speak it, it creates your desire.

CHAPTER TEN

PROVISION FOR HEALING

Is any sick among you? let him call for the elders of the church; and let them pray over him, anointing him with oil in the name of the Lord: And the prayer of faith shall save the sick, and the Lord shall raise him up; and if he have committed sins, they shall be forgiven him.

James 5:14-15

This scripture simply shows that it is not expected that anyone amongst God's people should be sick. But peradventure there is any that is sick; there is a provision in scriptures for his or her healing. There is power in the prayers of the saints. The power of God can heal any kind of sickness. The results that we generate on the altar of prayer are primarily dependent on the faithfulness of God. Our duty is to believe that God will honor his word. There is nothing in us humans, even as children of God that makes for supernatural healing. It is all about Jesus and the power of his word. He is too faithful to fail. The scripture says;

If we believe not, yet he abideth faithful: he cannot deny himself.

2 Timothy 2:13

He commanded us to call upon him any time we have problem in any area of our lives and he promised he will deliver us from that situation.

And call upon me in the day of trouble: I will deliver thee, and thou shalt glorify me.

Psalm 50:15

During his earthly ministry Jesus healed all manner of sickness.

And Jesus went about all Galilee, teaching in their synagogues, and preaching the gospel of the kingdom, and healing all manner of sickness and all manner of disease among the people. And his fame went throughout all Syria: and they brought unto him all sick people that were taken with divers diseases and torments, and those which were possessed with devils, and those which were lunatick, and those that had the palsy; and he healed them.

Matthew 4:23-2

When he was sending out his disciples for missions one of the instructions he gave to them was to heal the sick. This ensures that they are not the sick and that they continue with his mission even after he is gone.

Heal the sick, cleanse the lepers, raise the dead, cast out devils: freely ye have received, freely give.

Matthew 10:8

Healing did not end with the twelve disciples of Jesus as some people claim today. Jesus is still in the business of healing till today, setting people free from all forms of sicknesses, bondages and afflictions. The healing from God is free, you don't pay anything. Anyone that asks for monetary or any other form of reward is either working for his belly or he is working for the devil.

CHAPTER ELEVEN

HABITS FOR HEALTHY LIVING

In this chapter we will not be dealing with things like eating habits, exercise, not smoking and such like. However, it is expected that we should take good care of our health. In this chapter we will be taking a look at some of the salient, but latent things one can do to enhance his or her health and total well-being. It is not God that decides how healthy you are. He placed that responsibility in the hands of every individual. To begin with, God made it clear that He desires us to live in health. Whether we live in health or not, is up to us. God does not force it on anyone.

Beloved, I wish above all things that thou mayest prosper and be in health, even as thy soul prospereth

3 John 1:2

You need:

JOYFULNESS OF HEART

A merry heart doeth good like a medicine: but a broken spirit drieth the bones.

Proverbs 17:22

Joy is the ventilation of the spirit. Living a joyless life is like living in a poorly ventilated room, it can make you sick. Joy is indispensable if one desires to live healthy. Anything that tampers with your joy is indirectly tampering with your health. You need to maintain your joy at all cost. Joy is not the same with happiness. While happiness is condition dependent, that is, it is based on the happenings around you. Joy does not depend on the outcome of any event of your life. Joy is based on the promise of the scripture. It is important to mention at this point that joy is a fruit of the spirit. It is available to all but only those that are born of the spirit, that is, born again that can access it.

But the fruit of the Spirit is love, joy, peace, longsuffering, gentleness, goodness, faith, Meekness, temperance: against such there is no law.

Galatians 5:22-23

That is why I said earlier in the beginning chapter that salvation or being born again is our access to every blessing and promise of the scriptures. Listen to what the prophet Habakkuk said;

Although the fig tree shall not blossom, neither shall fruit be in the vines; the labour of the olive shall fail, and the fields shall yield no meat; the flock shall be cut off from the fold, and there shall be no herd in the stalls: Yet I will rejoice in the Lord, I will joy in the God of my salvation.

Habakkuk 3:17-18

Being joyful is a choice. You can choose to be joyful regardless of the condition of things around you. It is possible to rejoice always.

Rejoice in the Lord always: and again I say, Rejoice.

Philippians 4:4

It will take a deliberate effort to cultivate joy and live a lifestyle of joyfulness. You have to be intentional in your pursuit of a life of joy. You don't wait for someone else to make you feel joyful. All that you need to be joyful is within you. It is internal not external. Just make the decision to be joyful no matter what. A song writer says "Nothing gonna steal my joy". One of the treasures available in the wells of salvation is good health but it takes joy to draw from it.

Therefore with joy shall ye draw water out of the wells of salvation.

Isaiah 12:3

It is important to know that the happier you are, the healthier you live. To stay healthy one must stay merry hearted. So, no matter what is going on in your life, make the choice to stay happy. Stay away from people that break your joy.

THE NEED FOR REST

You don't need to be tired in order to rest. Rest is a mechanism designed by God to refresh the body. Rest is not the same with sleep although you do get rested in sleep. You don't necessarily have to lie down to sleep in order to get rested. You can sit or recline on a chair and get enough rest as you need. God, the creator of heaven and earth does not slumber nor sleep (Psalm 121:4), yet he rested (Genesis 2:2). You need to rest. For you to rest, you need to be calm and relax your mind. Put away electronics and phones. Turn off the TV set. Different people have different thresholds for rest. To some people, a quick twenty to thirty minutes or one hour rest is all they need in a day, and the body is refreshed, ready to go. Some others might need a little longer than that. By all means find time to rest. Practice it and it will surprise you what difference a little time of rest can make in your health. Rest refreshes your body and renews your strength. There are people that only rest during the time of holidays only. That should not be the case. Continuing in our work or whatever one does for a living without rest depletes the body resource. When a body is depleted it becomes groggy and vulnerable. This can make one susceptible to sickness. Many sicknesses can be avoided if only we can understand the vital role of rest to our total health and practice it. James Robinson said "Don't let your schedule run your life or it will ruin your life". The human body was not designed to run twenty-four seven or else it will crash. The truth is that all we think that we gain by not taking time to rest we lose to sickness when it strikes.

A wise man will hear, and will increase learning; and a man of understanding shall attain unto wise counsels:

Proverbs 1:5

Rest and be refreshed.

FERVENT PRAYERS

You need to pray fervently for your health and that of your family on daily basis. As a matter of fact, the title of this book came out of a line of prayer I pray every day. This time of prayer is not my quiet time with God. I pray this prayer in the bathroom. It is not a long time of prayer but it is a targeted prayer. Don't wait until sickness comes before you start praying. Pray to stop it from coming.

Confess your faults one to another, and pray one for another, that ye may be healed. The effectual fervent prayer of a righteous man availeth much.

James 5:16

OBSERVE THE LAW OF WORDS

It is important that we speak in line with the word of God. Do not say what God did not say about your life. You must make up your mind not to conform to the standard of this world. Don't be realistic, say only what you desire. It is a spiritual law that you are not permitted to experience what you cannot declare with your mouth. Words are spirits, and they are creative.

.... the words that I speak unto you, they are spirit, and they are life.

John 6:63

There is a direct correlation between the words you speak and how healthy you are.

What man is he that desireth life, and loveth many days, that he may see good? Keep thy tongue from evil, and thy lips from speaking guile.

Psalm 34:12-13

Speak the things that are right. Declare boldly that you cannot be sick. The lord has redeemed you from sickness.

Let the redeemed of the Lord say so, whom he hath redeemed from the hand of the enemy

Psalm 107:2

You don't owe anyone any apology. Some people will say to you; so and so are good Christians and they are sick. You are not so and so. Moreover, God does not deal with us as a group when it comes to our faith. He deals with us on individual basis. One of the ways to show what you believe is by the words you are speaking.

We having the same spirit of faith, according as it is written, I believed, and therefore have I spoken; we also believe, and therefore speak;

2 Corinthians 4:13

Declare it! "I shall never be sick again."

FINAL WORD

Do not miss the eternal glory for the few brief years of life here on earth. The most important thing in life is doing the will of God. It is time to set your priorities right. Listen to what Solomon said;

Let us hear the conclusion of the whole matter: Fear God, and keep his commandments: for this is the whole duty of man.

Ecclesiastes 12:13

Are you born again? I cannot conclude this writing without giving you the opportunity to make right your relationship with God. Say this short prayer and mean it with all your heart:

Lord Jesus, I come to you today just as I am. Forgive me my sins and wash me with your precious blood. I believe you died for me and rose again on the third day. I receive you right now into my heart as my Lord and personal savior. Thank you for saving me. I prayed in your precious name, Jesus. Amen!

Welcome to God's family.

Look for a Bible-believing and practicing church, join and be part of what God is doing in that local assembly of the saints. You can only be a fruitful child of God when you fellowship in the community of other believers.

Those that be planted in the house of the Lord shall flourish in the courts of our God.

Psalm 92:13

You Shall Never Be Sick Again!

OTHER BOOKS BY THE AUTHOR

The sex conspiracy

Divorce and Remarry (Man's Alternative, not God's Plan)

Purity for a Purpose

Made in the USA
Middletown, DE
25 January 2020